Billy Elliot

By Melvin Burgess

Based on a motion picture screenplay written by Lee Hall

LEVEL 1

SCHOLASTIC

'Billy Elliot' adapted by: Jacquie Bloese

Fact Files written by: Jane Rollason

Commissioning Editor: Jacquie Bloese

Editor: Jane Rollason

Cover layout: Emily Spencer

Designer: Sylvia Tate/Perry Tate Design

Picture research: Emma Bree

Photo credits: Cover image and film stills provided courtesy of Universal Studios. **Page 5:** Popperfoto, C. George/Alamy; PA/Empics. **Page 17:** Thinkstock/Alamy. **Page 32:** C. George/Alamy. **Page 33:** H. Ho/AFP/Getty Images; Thinkstock/Alamy. **Page 34:** Bettmann/Corbis. **Page 35:** Image100; J. Dittiger/Redferns/Alamy. **Page 36:** PA/Empics; Hemera; Stockbyte. **Page 37:** Big Box Of Art; Hemera; Photodisc. **Page 44:** PA/Empics; Big Box Of Art. **Page 45:** Hemera; Photodisc.

Published by Scholastic Ltd. 2005.

Mary Glasgow Magazines (Scholastic Ltd.)
Euston House
24 Eversholt Street
London NW1 1DB

Printed in Singapore. Reprinted in 2007, 2008, 2009 and 2010.
This edition printed in 2011.

Contents

page

Billy Elliot	**4–31**
People and places	**4**
Chapter 1: Billy: 'I love to boogie'	**6**
Chapter 2: Billy: Boys don't do ballet!	**8**
Chapter 3: Billy: Do the spin	**12**
Chapter 4: Jackie: My son Billy	**14**
Chapter 5: Billy: Just you and me	**15**
Chapter 6: Billy: Mam's dance	**18**
Chapter 7: Billy: Black Friday	**20**
Chapter 8: Tony: Happy Christmas!	**22**
Chapter 9: Billy: You're in trouble now	**25**
Chapter 10: Jackie: The scab bus	**26**
Chapter 11: Billy: A stupid dream	**28**
Chapter 12: Jackie: The letter	**30**
Epilogue: Jackie: Our Billy!	**31**
Fact Files	**32–37**
Ballet shoes!	**32**
Let's dance!	**34**
1984: the miners' strike	**36**
Self-Study Activities	**38–40**

Billy Elliot

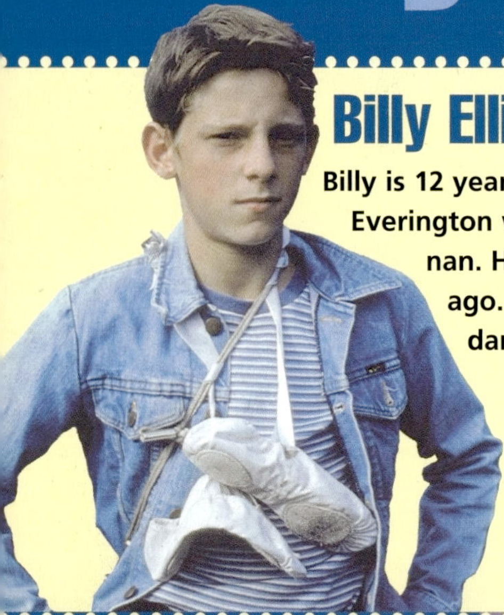

Billy Elliot

Billy is 12 years old. He lives in Everington with his dad, brother and nan. His mum died two years ago. He loves music and dancing.

Jackie Elliot

Billy's dad. He's a miner. He's on strike.

Tony Elliot

Billy's brother. He's 20 years old. He's a miner and he's on strike too. He hates the police and he hates scabs.

Mrs Wilkinson / 'Miss'

Billy's ballet teacher. She lives with her husband and daughter Debbie. She teaches ballet at the Social. The girls and Billy call her 'Miss'.

Michael

Billy's best friend.

Nan

Billy's grandmother. She's 80. She loved dancing when she was young.

Places

Everington is a mining town near Durham in the north-east of England. Most of the men here are miners.

The story starts in 1984. Mines are closing all over Britain. The miners are angry. They want to keep their jobs. There are no other jobs for the miners in Everington. They decide to go on strike.

But some miners still go to work. They want the money. The strikers call them 'scabs'.

The Social is a club for the people of Everington. They meet their friends here and have a beer. There are boxing lessons and ballet lessons at the Social.

Police and miners in 1984.

Billy and his family live in a street like this.

The Royal Ballet School is a big school in London. They teach ballet here.

Billy Elliot

Chapter 1 Billy: 'I love to boogie'

I hate my brother. He's stupid but he has got some good music. I listen to his music when he's out at work with my dad. Well – they're not at work, not now. They're on strike. But they still go to the mine every day.

Nan loves the music too. Tony and Dad leave in the morning, then the music goes on. I make breakfast for us and we both dance. I can hear her in her bedroom. She tries to dance but she can't walk very well now – well, she is eighty.

This morning, I made the eggs and danced to her bedroom.

'Hey, Nan! Breakfast!' I called. I opened the door with my foot and … Oh no! Not again! Her bed was empty.

I put the eggs on the kitchen table and ran out of the house. Where was she? She does this a lot. She forgets things – she forgets her name.

I looked up the street. 'Nan! NAN!' Which way? Then I had an idea. I ran to the end of the street and up to some trees. There she was. She often goes there. Why? Who knows? Maybe she played there when she was little. She looked frightened.

'Who are you?' she said.

'It's me, Nan. Billy!'

She didn't look very happy. Then we both heard something. Behind us ... on the road ... we saw them ... lots of them. The police. Their clothes were black and they had batons.

Nan looked at me. 'What are they?' she asked.

'Police, Nan. It's the police.'

'Are they here for us?' she asked.

'No, Nan. Not us.' I said.

'Is it Jackie? Is it Tony?' she asked. I didn't answer. I didn't want to know the answer. I took my nan's arm and we walked slowly home.

* * *

'I love to boogie / Jitterbug boogie ...' I'm trying to play 'Cosmic Boogie' on the piano and thinking about Mam*. It was her piano. Mam's dead. She died two years ago. I think about her a lot.

I've got a letter from her. She wrote it before she died. 'I'm still here, Billy,' she wrote. But she isn't here. She's dead.

Mam was good at the piano. She played for all of us. I'd like piano lessons but they're too expensive. We haven't got the money. My dad's always telling us that. We haven't got much. Not now that there's a strike.

'Billy! Stop that!'

It's Dad. He's going out again with Tony in a minute. Why do I have to stop? He's not going to be here!

'Why ...?' Then I say the wrong thing. 'If it was Mam ...'

Dad comes over. He closes the piano with a BANG!

'I'm not telling you again!'

I go to my room. Back to Tony's music ...

*Some people in the north of England say 'Mam'. People in the south say 'Mum'.

Chapter 2 Billy: Boys don't do ballet!

'Billy Elliot - this isn't a tea party – it's a boxing lesson! Hit him!'

It's Saturday morning and I'm at the boxing club at the Social. This morning, I'm against Greavesy and he's bigger than me. I have my own ideas about boxing. It's all about your feet. So, I run and turn and jump. I move quickly. Greavesy just stands there. George, the teacher, isn't happy.

'Hit him! Don't dance around!'

BANG! I'm on the floor. Greavesy's standing over me and he's smiling. I can hear George.

'Billy Elliot! Get up! You're going to do it right. You're not going home yet.'

I get up. George pulls me to the punchbag. 'Hit it! Your poor father. He pays for boxing lessons. And this happens!' And on ... and on ... and on ...

I'm angry now. I hit the punchbag. I hate the punchbag.

* * *

'Arms up. And one – and two and three and four. Feel the music.'

On the other side of the room, there's a ballet class. Someone's playing the piano. One and two and three and four. As the music plays, I hit the punchbag.

'One and two.' And bang and hit. 'And three and four.' And hit and bang.

'That's better,' George says. 'Stay here and get it right. See you next week.'

And he goes out. All the other boys go too.

'Right, girls. And … one and two. Debbie – don't look at me. Look in front of you! And three … and four …'

I go and watch. It's clever. They all dance together. Left and two, and down and two, and turn and two. I try it. I stretch out my leg. Yeah – easy!

'Why don't you try?'

It's Debbie. She goes to my school.

'Nah,' I say. Boys don't do ballet!

'Legs up!'

They all stretch their legs. Mrs Wilkinson – she's the teacher - walks around and looks closely at each leg.

I try it. Debbie laughs at me. 'Your leg's moving!'

I look down. She's right. 'I'm wearing boxing shoes,' I tell her.

Mrs Wilkinson takes a cigarette from her pocket. She smokes a lot. 'OK, girls. And ... one and two and three and four.'

I want to do it too. I try but it's difficult. I start to listen to the music. It's easier then.

'Shoes off!' Miss is in front of me.

'Not me, Miss …' I start to say - but she's already walking down the room. I take off my shoes and then she's back again – with ballet shoes.

'Here you are,' she says, 'You can't dance in boxing shoes.'

I don't know, but then I think 'Why not?'

* * *

So, I do it. I do ballet for the first time. It isn't easy but Miss is a good teacher. We're all standing on one leg with the other leg behind. Miss comes over.

'I like the leg,' she says, and then walks off. She doesn't say much but I'm happy.

* * *

I'm walking home later and Miss drives by. She sees me and stops the car. Debbie's sitting in the back. Oh, I think, Debbie's her daughter!

Miss is still smoking. She looks at me. 'It's 50p a lesson, you know. Bring me the money next week.'

'I can't. I'm going to boxing.'

'You're terrible at boxing!' says Debbie, and laughs.

'Be quiet!' Miss looks around at Debbie and then back at me. 'Didn't you enjoy it today?'

I don't say anything.

'It's your life,' she says and off they go.

Miss was right. I enjoyed it but the music was a bit boring. I think about Fred Astaire. My nan loves him. He can dance! I want to dance like him. I run and jump down the road. Fred Astaire's music is playing in my head and I feel great!

Chapter 3 Billy: Do the spin

I think about ballet all the time. One and two and up and down. Miss's words and the music are always in my head. But there's a problem - I feel stupid! And then there's my dad. And Tony! Miners don't do ballet. Miners' sons don't do ballet. Miners don't do much when they're on strike.

The strike is going to end soon. I heard it on the TV. The cold weather's coming. The strikers and their families are going to be cold and hungry. They're going to need money. The strike is going to be over by Christmas.

People know about the ballet at school but I don't care. Some of the boys laugh at me.

'Hey, Billy! Where are your pink ballet shoes today?'

What do they know? Debbie Wilkinson's always talking to me too. She and her mam are posh – not like my family. She walked home with me from school the other day.

'Lots of boys do ballet, you know,' she said.

'Don't be stupid. Who? Who do we know?'

'No one here but lots of men do it. Are you coming next week?' She looked at me.

'I'm going to boxing. My dad says,' I said. I was a bit angry.

'OK.' She walked off. She lives in the nice part of town. In a posh house with a posh garden. Her and her mam don't know anything about our life. Then the music comes back in my head. I start to dance. And I forget about my life too.

* * *

I've got this friend, Michael. He hates football – not like me. We're different but we're best friends. I can talk to him about things. I told him about the ballet. I did some of the moves. He thinks it's cool.

'Leg out, arm out, one two!' I said. 'Eyes to the front.'

Michael laughed. 'When's the next lesson?'

'I'm not going,' I said. 'Ballet's for girls. I feel stupid.'

'You are stupid!' Michael laughed. 'Anyway, it's not just for girls. It's different for men. Men are stronger.'

He was right. I can jump higher than the girls in the ballet class. And I'm better than most of them.

So I went again. On Saturday, I took my 50p from the kitchen table and I went to the Social. This week, the class was in a different room. That was good because I didn't want to see George.

At the start, it was boring. I didn't know the moves. So I stopped. Miss came over.

'What are you doing?'

'I don't know the moves, Miss,' I said.

'Follow the girls. Go to the back and watch them. And ... one, two, three.'

That was OK but it was still a bit boring. Then Miss showed us the spin. You spin around and around very fast and then you stop. You must stay in the same place. It looks great but it's very difficult. You fall on the floor a lot. We all tried it.

'Do it at home,' Miss said, 'Try again and again. You can do it.'

At the end of the class, Miss came over to me. 'So, are you coming next week?'

'I don't know, Miss.'

She looked at my ballet shoes. 'Give me those, then.'

I didn't want to. I wanted to learn the spin and do it at boxing. I wanted to see George's face!

'No, it's OK,' I said and I gave her my 50p.

She took it and went off. She didn't say anything.

At home, Nan was in the kitchen.

'Ballet shoes! How lovely!' she said.

'Don't tell Dad!' I said and ran into my room. Luckily, Dad and Tony were out. Dad is NOT going to understand about ballet shoes. Dad isn't going to understand about any of this.

I put the ballet shoes under my bed with my boxing things. Anyway, I'm going to go to boxing soon. I'm going to go when I can do the spin …

Chapter 4 Jackie: My son Billy

There's something funny about Billy at the moment. He's a bit different from the other boys – I know that. But now, it's this 'spinning'.

He does it everywhere. He puts out his arms and spins around and around. He looks a bit stupid. Like a girl! He doesn't care – not Billy.

'It's a boxing move,' he tells me.

Boxing! Sometimes, I can't believe Billy is my son.

Then, there's the strike. We started four months ago. We're so poor now. We haven't got money for anything.

What's going to happen? We don't know. Maybe they're going to close the mines. Maybe they decided a long time ago. So why are we doing this? Tony's angry. I see it in his eyes – every day at the mine. What's he going to do if there's no mine?

Some men choose to work. We call them 'scabs'. The strikers stand together at the mine. The scabs go through in buses. There are police everywhere. We shout at the buses. We bang on the windows. The scabs look frightened. I'm not surprised.

This morning, I was next to George. It was cold. We waited for the scab buses.

'Listen, Jackie,' he said, 'Forget the money – the 50p for the boxing. I don't do it for the money.'

'What?!' I didn't understand.

'It's Billy. He doesn't come to boxing now. Is it because of the money?'

I started to think. Where did Billy go every Saturday morning?

Then a bus came in and everyone started to shout.

'SCAB! SCAB! SCAB!'

I shouted with the other men but I thought about other things. Tomorrow was Saturday. Billy's boxing day. I had an idea ...

Chapter 5 Billy: Just you and me

I can spin now! I can do everything – all the moves. Miss teaches me for a lot of the lesson. The girls aren't happy about it.

'Miss – what about us?' they say.

She doesn't listen. 'I'm busy!'

Then it happened. Michael often said to me, 'What about your dad? What are you going to do?'

Yeah, it happened. I was in the centre of the class. Miss was next to me.

'And stretch your leg, Billy.'

I looked up and there he was by the door. His face was red. Miss saw him too. The music stopped.

'You! Out! Now!' he shouted.

Miss wanted to say something but I stopped her. I had enough problems. I followed Dad out of the Social.

* * *

'Ballet!'

We were in the kitchen. Dad didn't speak to me when we left the Social. Maybe he was too angry – I don't know.

'What's wrong with ballet?' I said. 'Lots of people do it.'

Dad's face was red again.

'Lots of GIRLS do ballet, Billy. Not boys! Boys do football or boxing.'

It was true in a way. Ballet isn't boxing. You don't hit anyone. It's not mining. So my dad can't understand it.

So it's not boxing or mining. Well, so what? I'm not the same as my dad. I can be different.

'I like dancing, Dad. That's all it is – dancing. Why's that so bad?'

'Listen, forget about dancing! You're not doing it! Understand?'

I jumped up and shouted in his face, 'I hate you!' I ran out of the house. I ran and ran. I hated my dad. I loved dancing and I was good at it. I knew that. Miss knew it too. Suddenly, I wanted to see her.

* * *

I was in Miss's house. It was funny. Me, Debbie, Miss and her husband. He was funny too. He was always in the pub, Debbie said. He always had a beer in his hand.

'Oh, it's little Gene Kelly,' he said when he saw me.

'Be quiet, Tom,' Miss said. 'You're not in the pub now.'

I had dinner with them. Later, Miss took me home in her car. She stopped near my house and looked at me.

'Billy, I'm thinking about the Royal Ballet School.'

'Aren't you a bit old, Miss?' I said.

'Not me! You! There's an audition in Newcastle*. In two weeks.'

Ballet school? Me? Ballet - all day, every day ...

'Can you do ballet as a job then, Miss?' I asked her.

'Yes, if you're good enough.'

'But I don't know anything.'

'Look.' She took a cigarette from her bag. 'They teach you. It's a school. And ...' She waited a minute.' I think you're good enough.'

Wow! She didn't usually say anything nice.

'What about my dad?'

'I can speak to him if you want.'

'No! Please, Miss.' I knew my dad.

'I can give you more lessons,' she said, 'Just you and me. Don't think about the money. I'm not doing it for the money.'

I thought about it. My dad didn't know about it and that was wrong. But I wanted to be a dancer.

I smiled at Miss, 'OK, then.'

*A big city in the north-east of England.

She smiled too. She didn't usually smile.

'Six o'clock on Monday at the Social,' she said.

'OK,' I opened the car door.

'Oh, and Billy. Bring something with you. Something that's important to you. We must think of an idea for the audition dance.'

Chapter 6 Billy: Mam's dance

There wasn't much time - the audition was in two weeks. I met Miss almost every night. 'I'm going to Michael's house,' I told Dad.

The first evening, I had some things with me. My football. Some T. Rex music – 'I like to boogie'. It was Tony's. I didn't ask him. Then there was the letter from my mam.

Miss started to read the letter. 'Dear Billy.' She stopped. 'Can I read this, Billy?'

'Yeah,' I said.

' "I'm still here, Billy. You can't see me. But I am. I'm always with you. Don't forget that. And I love you. Be true to Billy Elliot, all your life." '

Miss looked away and didn't say anything.

'Are you OK, Miss?' I asked. 'She's going to cry,' I thought.

'She was a very special person, Billy,' she said.

'Nah – she was just my mam,' I said.

'What did your mam like doing?' she asked me.

'She liked music,' I said, and then we listened to the T. Rex music.

'I like to boogie
Jitterbug boogie
I like to boogie
On a Saturday night.'

'It's happy music,' Miss said, 'Dance music. And your mam liked this?'

'Aye*.'

'Then this is our dance, Billy. Let's go!'

We danced and jumped and ran around. We thought of lots of new moves.

'Now, think about your mam,' Miss said. 'She's watching you. She's smiling and laughing.'

And it worked! I thought about mam and I did a great spin. I was on top of the world!

* * *

At home, things were very different. No one was on top of the world. There were police all over the town. They frightened me.

Tony was never frightened. He shouted a lot at Dad.

'What's wrong with you?! This strike is our only hope!' Dad didn't answer. He just sat there and said nothing. I was sorry for him.

* * *

Tonight, I'm in bed, and I hear something in the kitchen. It's Dad and Tony. I sit up and listen. Tony sounds very angry.

'I'm not going to sit at home and do nothing!!' he shouts. 'You think it's the end, but for me, it's the start. Now, move!'

I run into the kitchen. Tony has a baton – a police baton. Where did he get that? What's he going to do with it?

This time, Dad shouts back, 'You're not going! And you're not going to use that.' He's looking at the baton.

*Some people in the north say 'Aye' for 'Yes', specially in Scotland. Billy's dad comes from Scotland.

'Forget about the police! They're doing a job – that's all.'

'Try and stop me, then!' says Tony. 'You can't do anything. You're nothing. Without Mam, you're NOTHING!'

They're by the back door. Dad's face is white. Suddenly he hits Tony. CRACK! Tony falls to the floor.

'Stop it! Stop it!' I shout.

Tony gets up slowly. He doesn't say a word. He doesn't look at Dad. He just runs out of the door. The baton is under his arm. Dad doesn't stop him this time.

Chapter 7 Billy: Black Friday

'Billy! You're not trying! Arm up!'

'What?'

I'm at the Social with Miss but I can only think about last night and my dad and Tony.

'Eyes to the front!'

BANG! Dad hits Tony.

'Do it again, Billy!'

BANG! Tony's on the floor.

'Billy, that's not good enough!'

'I can't!'

Suddenly I hate her.

She's standing right next to me and smoking in my face.

'Do it again!' she says.

'No!'

'What?!' She can't believe it.

Suddenly, I am angry about everything. Last night, the audition. Everything's going wrong. Tony was right about one thing. Without Mam, we're all nothing. And she's never coming back.

I run out of the room. Miss follows me.

'Billy, I'm sorry,' she says. 'I want to help you.'

'No, you don't. The audition's for you – not for me.'

'That's not true!' she says.

I can't stop now. 'What have you got? Nothing. No dance school. What are you? You're nothing!'

'Don't speak to me like that!' Then, she hits me across the face. She looks very surprised. I'm surprised too!

I want to run. But … I can't leave. I must dance. And because I can't leave, I start to cry.

She puts out her arms. 'I'm sorry, Billy.'

And I cry in her arms for about five minutes. I can't stop.

'Right,' she says. 'Is that enough?'

'Yes,' I say. 'Sorry, Miss.'

'Right, then,' she says. 'Let's start again.'

* * *

There was something different about that Friday. Black Friday, Dad called it. The audition was the next morning.

I walked home after my last lesson with Miss. I was happy. I did my audition dance in my head. Then I turned into our road … and saw them all. There were police everywhere.

Mrs Watts lives near us. She saw me and pulled me into her house.

'Get in, Billy!'

'What's happening?'

'It's your* Tony. He's in trouble. The police want him.'

*In the north people sometimes say 'your Billy' or 'our Tony'; it means the person is in your family.

Tony! I didn't understand. Where did he go at night? What did he do?

My Dad and Tony – specially Tony – hate the police. Now, I understand.

I saw one man. He was in front of one of the police. The policeman hit him with his baton. He didn't stop. He hit him again and again.

Then I saw our* Tony. He ran up the road with the police all around him. They were faster than him. I ran to the door.

'Tony! In here!' He didn't hear me. It was too loud – everyone shouted, batons banged on doors.

After that, I saw about twenty police – all together. And our Tony was under them …

Chapter 8 Tony: Happy Christmas!

I stayed in the police station that night. There was no bed. 'Where do I sleep?' I asked. They laughed. I was black and blue. I hate the police.

Next morning I sat in the courtroom. There was a big policeman next to me. I saw Dad and our Billy. Dad was angry but he didn't say anything. It was over very quickly.

Pay the court one hundred pounds, they said. We haven't got any money. They know that.

'And a happy Christmas to you too,' I shouted.

'Get out of here!' said the policeman.

We walked home - me, Dad and Billy. I wanted to get home and go to bed. I wanted to cry like a little boy. But there was this woman, in front of our house.

'Who's that?' I asked. She came up to Billy. Did she know him?

'Where were you, Billy? What happened?'

Billy didn't want to say anything. But she waited.

'Our Tony was in court,' he said quietly. 'I went too.' He didn't look at her.

Our dad looked at Billy and this woman. Did he know her too? 'What's going on?' I thought.

'Let's go in,' Dad said.

'What's all this about?' I said. I didn't want this. Things were bad enough. I didn't like this woman. She was posh. She had posh clothes. She wasn't like us.

We went into the living room. Billy didn't look very happy. 'He's in trouble,' I thought. Then she started.

'Today, Billy had an audition for the Royal Ballet School. I know things are difficult but ...'

I didn't believe my ears. I laughed. I looked at Billy and laughed again.

'What?! Ballet?!' I said.

I went over to the woman and shouted in her face.

'My brother does not do ballet, you stupid woman! My brother is not going to do ballet!'

Her face was white. She was frightened but she didn't move.

'Don't shout at me,' she said. 'Billy's a very good dancer. Where does he go after school every day? You don't know and you don't care.'

I wanted to hit her. She knew but she didn't care.

'Is Billy going to be like you?' she said to me. 'No job, no hope? Do you want that for Billy?'

'He's not going to be a scab,' I shouted. 'Look at him. He's only 12. He's a child. And you're putting stupid ideas in his head.'

'You learn better when you're young,' said Billy.

'Shut it!' I shouted at him. I turned back to her. 'My brother is not running around in a stupid dress for you or anyone.'

'It's not for me,' she said. 'It's for Billy.' And then she turned to Billy. 'See you, Billy!' she said and walked out of the house.

'Get out of our house!' I shouted at her. 'And don't come back!' She didn't hear.

I wanted to hit Billy then. I wanted to hit someone. But he was behind our dad.

'Shut up! I hate you!' he shouted at me. I looked at him. 'He's right – he hates me,' I thought.

'You little …' I tried to hit him, but Dad stopped me. Billy ran out of the back door.

I looked at Dad. 'I'm going to the pub,' I said. I banged the door on my way out. And if I see that posh woman again …

Chapter 9 Billy: You're in trouble now

'That was the worst Christmas of my life!' I said. I was with Michael. It was the day after Christmas and we were out in the cold.

'No Christmas tree, no nothing!' And no Mam.

'Have some of this.' He had some of his dad's beer. I tried it.

'Yeuch! I don't like it,' I said.

'What do you want to do then?' asked Michael.

'Let's go to the Social!'

'Why?' Michael asked, 'There's no one there now.'

'So let's go!' I said and we went.

* * *

Michael and I were in the boxing club.

'OK,' I said, 'You're the girl. Up and one and two.'

We did some of the moves together. It was good to dance again. Suddenly, Michael stopped.

'What is it?' I looked at the door. It was my dad. This time, I didn't want to run. I didn't care.

I walked over to him. I looked at him. And then I did my audition dance. I jumped and spun. I wanted to show Dad everything. When I finished, he didn't say anything.

He looked at me and ran out of the room.

'Billy, what did you do that for?' said Michael. 'You're in big trouble now!'

He was right but, well, that was Billy Elliot. Billy Elliot dances. That was me.

Chapter 10 Jackie: The scab bus

I'm almost running down that road. Billy … our Billy. He's good at something – no, not good … fantastic! Now, I don't know much about ballet. It's for posh people – like that Mrs Wilkinson. But maybe … just maybe …

My head's spinning and I'm thinking about my Sarah. My wife. I can almost hear her.

'Help the boy, Jackie! What's wrong with you?! He's our son.'

She's right. That Mrs Wilkinson is right too. I'm going to see her – now.

* * *

Her husband opens the door. He looks at me.

'In there,' he says.

I go into the living room. There she is with her cigarettes.

'How much is it going to cost?' I ask her.

'Happy Christmas to you too!' she says, then she smiles. 'Sit down.'

'I'm OK.' I don't want to stay for long. 'How much?'

'For the audition? The cost of the bus to London and a hotel for the night. I can help …'

'I don't want your money!' I say. 'How good is he?'

She smokes her cigarette and looks at me. 'He's the best, Mr Elliot.'

'Thanks.' I leave. I need time. I must think.

What can I do? But I already know the answer.

* * *

It's six o'clock in the morning, and I'm waiting for the bus with the other men. It's the scab bus.

I'm doing it for Billy. I must help him – he's my son.

I didn't sleep last night … I'm doing it for one week. One week's money for our Billy's audition.

Our Tony doesn't know. No one knows yet. Only the other scabs.

The bus comes and we all get on. No one speaks as we drive there. When we arrive, I can hear the men. 'Scab, scab, scab!' they shout.

I know the words. I shouted them last week ...

We drive through the men. BANG, BANG, BANG! They bang on the bus windows. The police try to stop them. The bus stops. Their faces are so close. I'm very frightened now. I look around me. Some of the scabs put their hands over their faces. Not me. I don't care. I look out of the window and then I see him. It's Tony. He's looking back at me. He can't believe his eyes. I don't know what to do. HE CAN'T BELIEVE HIS EYES. The bus moves on.

* * *

'Dad, Dad! What are you doing?'

I'm off the bus. I'm going to go into the mine. And there he is – our Tony. He's calling to me. He's like a little boy again. I go over to him.

'I'm sorry, son. It's for Billy,' I say and then I start to cry.

'You can't go back, Dad. Not now.' Tony looks at me and he's crying too.

'There's another way, Dad. We can help Billy. Please!'

* * *

So, I didn't go into the mine. I went home with our Tony. I told him all about Billy and the ballet.

'We're going to find that money, Dad,' he said. 'Billy's going to the audition.'

Tony had to be strong. I wasn't – not now.

Chapter 11 Billy: A stupid dream

I'm on a bus to London with my dad. I can't believe it. Wasn't it all a stupid dream – me and the Royal Ballet School? But people in the town helped with the money. We had a dance at the Social ... and then, there were some of my mam's things. 'I'm going to sell them,' Dad said one morning. I don't want to think about that.

* * *

I hated the Royal Ballet School when I saw it. It was so big and posh.

'How much is this going to cost?!' Dad said.

I changed into my dance clothes. There were other boys there. They were posh too. They didn't understand my English.

'Sorry?' 'What did you say?'

'Oh, shut it!'

Then there was the audition. There were five people from the Royal Ballet School there. They sat behind a long table. They didn't like me.

'Do you have some music, Billy?' I gave it to them.

T. Rex. It wasn't right for that place. I know that now.

I didn't dance. I didn't move. I just looked at them. Then, I heard Miss in my ear.

'Billy, you're not trying. Go on – just do it!'

So, I did it – badly. When I finished, nobody said anything. They wrote some things down. Then one of them said, 'Thank you, Billy. You can go now.'

I almost ran out of there. All that work, all that money – for nothing. I just wanted to go home.

* * *

But it wasn't over. They called me and Dad into the audition room again. We sat in front of that long table.

'Now, Billy, we have some questions for you,' one of them said, 'Why do you like ballet?'

I didn't answer. I wasn't right for this place.

'Don't know,' I said.

'Well, what do you like about dancing?'

Dad looked at me.

'Um. Everything.'

'He dances all the time,' my dad said.

'Yes, we've got a letter from Mrs Wilkinson here. And you, Mr Elliot, do you like ballet?'

'Um, well I don't know much about it,' Dad said.

Well, that was true. And that was about it.

We got up and walked to the door.

'One more thing, Billy,' said a very posh woman. 'How do you feel when you dance?'

I thought for a minute.

'I feel good,' I started. 'When I dance, I forget the world and the strike and everything. There's fire in my body. It's like … it's like flying.'

That sounded stupid, I thought.

Chapter 12 Jackie: The letter

Poor Billy. When we got home, he went to bed. He didn't want any dinner. He didn't want to talk.

And that place … It was a different world. All those rich boys. Special dancing lessons. Big houses. Posh cars. It wasn't us …

But … the Royal Ballet people. Maybe they weren't so bad. When we left the audition room, one of the teachers said, 'Good luck with the strike, Mr Elliot.'

* * *

We waited one week. Two weeks. Then the letter arrived. Billy was at school. It was a long day. Billy came home at four o'clock. We were all there.

Billy took the letter. No one said anything. He went into his nan's room, and closed the door. Then … nothing. He didn't come out. In the end, we went in there. I opened the door. Billy started to cry.

'I did it,' he said quietly, 'I'm in.'

* * *

YEEESSSS! I ran up the road to the Social. He did it! Our Billy! I wanted to tell everyone. I ran into the Social.

'He's in! He did it!'

Nobody answered.

'It's over, Jackie. We're going back.'

'What?'

'The strike's over. We're going back to work on Monday.'

* * *

So that was it. The mine didn't stay open very long after that. That was ten years ago, now. It was the end for me. But life is only just starting for Billy. And that's something!

Epilogue Jackie: Our Billy!

Well, London doesn't change. It's still big. It's still expensive but we didn't pay for our ballet tickets. I'm sitting here with our Tony. It's funny to see your name in big letters. There – on the front of the Royal Opera House.

'The Royal Ballet. Billy Elliot.' Our Billy.

Then the music starts. And there he is. He runs on and … jumps. What a jump! No one does it like Billy. He spins and spins. Everyone's watching. He's the best!

And he's smiling all the time. He's smiling at us.

So, I stand up and I shout, 'Billy! Billy Elliot!'

Tony's standing with me,'Our Billy!' he shouts.

And other people stand up too. And, you know, I'm never going to forget this. It's the best time of my life!

The end

Ballet Shoes!

Use your dictionary for new words.

Q Who started the Royal Ballet School?
A A famous dancer called Ninette de Valois, in 1926.

Q Which famous dancers went there?
A Dame Margot Fonteyn, Wayne Sleep and Darcey Bussell.

Q How old are the students?
A They start at 11 and leave when they're 18.

Q Do they just do ballet and dance?
A No. They have school lessons too and they take the same exams as other schools.

Q Where is the school?
A The school for the younger students is in a beautiful park in London called Richmond Park (Billy and his dad come here for the audition).

Q Where do the older students go?
A The Upper School for 16- to 18-year-olds is cool – it's in Covent Garden, right in the centre of London. It's next door to the Royal Opera House. The Royal Ballet dance here.

Q Do the students dance at the ROH?
A Yes, in their last year.

Q Who can study here?
A Anyone… if they can dance like Billy!

It's not easy!

Ballet dancers are very strong and very fit. They work hard every day. They can't have lots of holidays. And they are never happy with their bodies. 'I don't like my feet.' 'My legs are too short.' 'My arms are too fat.' Dancers are also very thin, specially the girls. Some young dancers have eating problems and they get too thin. Ballet is hard work for your body. You can be a dancer at 17 or 18, but most dancers only work for 20 years. Then you are too old and you must find a different job.

Jumping

When people go to the ballet, they want to see big jumps. Some people can do this. Some people can't. Your bones must be right.

Do you know any famous dancers? Who are they? What kind of dance do they do?

Alicia Markova: Famous at 14!

Born: Lilian Alice Marks, December 1910, north London.

Life change: One day, when she was 8, her mother said, 'Your feet are flat.' She took her to ballet classes. Lilian's life changed on that day.

From London to Monte Carlo: Diaghilev was a Russian with a big dance group. He was in London and he saw Lilian. 'This child is going to be a star!' he said. He took her to join his dance group in Monte Carlo in 1925.

Name change: Diaghilev changed Lilian's name to Alicia Markova (he didn't ask her first!)

First big dance: She danced the most important part in *Le Rossignol* in Paris in 1925 when she was only 14! Alicia Markova was soon very famous.

Dancing life: She danced all around the world. She stopped dancing when she was 50. After that she was a teacher.

What do these words mean?
exam fit fat thin bones

Let's dance!

Some people say, 'The British can't dance!' Is that true? Maybe, but they still love dancing. So who cares? These dances were all in fashion in the UK in the last 100 years. Use your dictionary to find new words.

Time: the 1920s
Dance: **THE CHARLESTON**
Music: jazz, ragtime

This dance came to the UK from South Carolina in the US. It came with shorter skirts and shorter hair for women. British girls loved it. Their mothers hated it. It's a very fast dance. You flap your arms and kick your legs out.

Time: the 1950s
Dance: **JIVING**
Music: rock 'n' roll, Elvis

Rock 'n' roll came to Britain with Bill Haley's film, *Rock Around the Clock*. When British teenagers saw it in cinemas, they started dancing! They danced everywhere – in the cinemas, in the streets … You do this dance with a partner. The women wear big skirts. The men wear straight trousers and soft shoes.

Time: the 1960s
Dance: **THE TWIST**
Music: the Beatles

This easy dance started with the Beatles music. One of their songs is called 'Twist and Shout'. You twist your hips in time to the music. You can do this dance with someone or on your own.

Time: the 1980s
Dance: **BREAKDANCING**
Music: electro music, Rock Steady Crew

Breakdancing started with James Brown in the 1960s and his song 'One Good Foot'. He got down on the floor and did moves with his feet. People loved it. Then everyone forgot about it. It came back in the 1980s and they called it breakdancing. You change your move when there's a break in the music. It has very difficult moves.

Time: the 1990s
Dance: **TECHNO/DANCE**
Music: Kraftwerk, synthesizers, drum machines and sampled music (bits from lots of different music played together)

This started with disco in the 1970s. Big sounds, lots of coloured lights and fast music. In the 1980s teenagers went to raves and danced to house music all night. Raves were in big, old, empty buildings. There are lots of types of dance music – trance, techno, ambient, house …

Time: the 2000s
Dance: **MOSHING**
Music: rock, punk and metal

You mosh in a mosh pit in front of the band. You jump up and bang into other people. They bang into you. You wear shoes with hard tops and a T-shirt with the band's name on.

Can you do any of these dances? What dances do you do in your country? Did your parents do any of these dances?

What do these words mean?

flap hips kick soft straight

1984: THE MINERS

The story of Billy Elliot happens in 1984 in a small mining town in the north of England. They mine coal here. The miners' strike was a very important time in Britain.

The strike started in March 1984. The government wanted to close 20 coal mines. About 20,000 miners worked at these mines. Some miners wanted to keep the jobs. But some miners didn't want to go on strike. The government and the police kept the mines open. After one year, the strikers went back to work. And then the mines started to close.

1984: I was there

The scab's daughter

"My dad didn't go on strike. He didn't think it was right. He worked. At first I went to school. But the other children shouted 'Scab' at me and took all my schoolbooks. The teachers didn't help me. I was frightened, so I stayed at home. My friends didn't speak to me. After the strike, we moved to another town."

The student

"I was a student in London. I went up to the north one weekend. I wanted to help the miners. But the police got me. 'Only strikers can stand on the picket line,' the law said. They took me to court. Two hundred pounds, it cost me. So I went back to London."

STRIKE

- In 1984 230,000 miners worked in the coal mines in England and Wales. Today, there are 7,000 miners.
- In 1984 there were 170 mines open. Today, there are 9.

Where is your electricity going to come from?

Coal is bad for the world. It makes CO_2 and CO_2 makes global warming faster. What other things can we use?

- We use coal to make electricity. Where does your electricity come from now?
- Where is it going to come from when you're 30 years old?

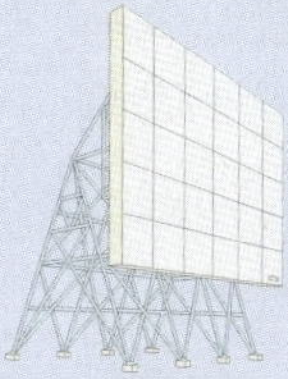

... the sun?

... the wind?

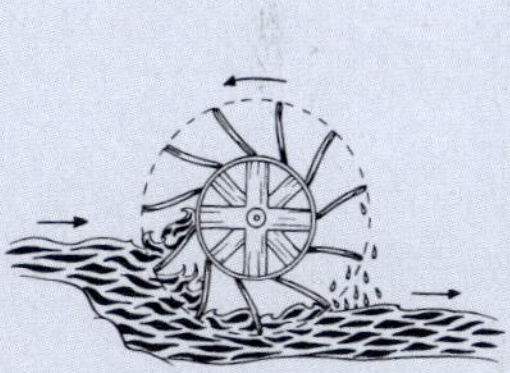

... the sea?

Are there often strikes in your country? What are they about?

What do these words mean? You can use your dictionary.

coal government kept (*past of* keep) picket line law electricity global warming

The striker's son

"There was nothing to eat. At Christmas we got one thing each. Some miners in Germany gave us footballs! And we got Christmas lunch from France. That was great!"

The policeman

"It was hard work. We left home on Sunday and got back on Friday night. We stayed in an empty school. We got to the picket line before the sun came up. First the strikers arrived. They shouted at us. Then the scabs arrived. We took them into the mine. A lot of us were sorry for the strikers. But you can't break the law."

Chapters 1 – 4

Before you read

Use a dictionary for this section.

1 Match the verbs and nouns.

play **hit** **bang** **smoke** **drink**

punchbag **beer** **cigarette** **piano** **drum**

2 Do you do boxing or ballet? Which do you like better?

3 Choose the right verb.

spin **jump** **go on strike** **stretch**

a) When you ... you go up in the air.
b) When you ... you go around and around.
c) When you ... you make your body long.
d) When you ... you stop work.

4 Answer the questions.

a) Does a miner work in the dark or in the light?
b) Who uses a baton in their job? A police officer, a miner or a ballet dancer?
c) What happens on Christmas Day in your house?
d) Who is stronger – your mum or your dad?
e) Do posh people wear cheap clothes or expensive clothes?

After you read

5 Read People and places on pages 4-5.

a) How many people live in Billy's house? Who are they?
b) What can children and teenagers do for fun at the Social?
c) The miners are on strike. Why do some miners still go to work?

6 Who …
   a) would like piano lessons?
   b) doesn't want to hear the piano?
   c) is better at boxing – Billy or Greavesy?
   d) smokes all the time?
   e) was Fred Astaire?
   f) says, 'The miner's strike is going to be over by Christmas'?
   g) thinks ballet is cool?

7 What do you think?
Is it cool for boys to do ballet?

Chapters 5 – 8

Before you read

8 Find the best word for these spaces. Use your dictionary.
trouble   court   audition
   a) I want to be Juliet in the school play. The … is tomorrow. I hope I get the part.
   b) Some men took a lot of money from the bank. The police got them. They're going to be in … tomorrow.
   c) My brother didn't go to school for a week. He and his friend went into town every day. He's in … now.

9 Jackie learns from George that Billy isn't going to boxing. What's Jackie going to do, do you think?

After you read

10 Answer the questions.
   a) How does Jackie feel when he sees Billy in the ballet class?
   b) Why does Mrs Wilkinson want Billy to audition for the Royal Ballet?
   c) How does Mrs Wilkinson feel when she reads Billy's mam's letter?
   d) Why are Tony and Jackie shouting in the kitchen at four o'clock in the morning?

e) Why is Billy angry with Mrs Wilkinson in his lesson?
f) Why doesn't Billy go to the audition?
g) What does Tony think of Mrs Wilkinson?

11 You are Mrs Wilkinson. Write about meeting Billy's family. Use the present tense.

12 What do you think?
You play the guitar in a band. That's all you want to do. Your family don't like it. They don't think it's a good job. What do you do?

Chapters 9 – Epilogue

Before you read

13 Which of these things is going to happen, do you think?
a) Billy is going to stop dancing.
b) Mrs Wilkinson is going to stop Billy's lessons.
c) Tony is going to go back to work and be a scab.
d) Jackie is going to change his ideas about ballet for boys.

After you read

14 Put these events in order.
a) A letter arrives.
b) Billy and Jackie go to the audition in London.
c) Billy gets into the Royal Ballet.
d) Billy shows Jackie his audition dance.
e) Jackie decides to work for a week.
f) Jackie is going into the mine but Tony stops him.
g) Jackie sees Michael and Billy dancing at the Social.
h) They think it goes badly.

15 What do you think?
Billy follows his dream and he gets there. Can anyone follow their dream?
Why/why not?